Introduction

Our bodies have been constructed to withstand an enormous amount of pressure. God has made us to be fairly resilient people. We can survive the heat of the tropics or the icy winds of winter. With undaunted courage we can go through seasons of illness, financial reversals, domestic disappointments, unemployment, or the death of someone dear to us . . . *if*. If we don't lose the one essential ingredient—hope.

We can rebound against wind and weather, calamity and tragedy, disease and death, so long as we have our hope. We can live weeks without food, days without water, and even several minutes without air, but take away our hope and within the briefest amount of time, *we toss in the towel!*

Knowing that that is true about His creatures, God calls hope the "anchor of the soul," the irreplaceable, irreducible source of determination. He not only calls it our "anchor," He develops a helpful series of thoughts about hope in His Book, the Bible. But in one special section of Scripture, He concentrates direct attention upon this subject. That particular section is the major emphasis of this booklet.

For when God made the promise to Abraham, since He could swear by no one greater, He swore by Himself, saying, "I will surely bless you, and I will surely multiply you." And thus, having patiently waited, he obtained the promise. For men swear by one greater than themselves, and with them an oath given as confirmation is an end of every dispute. In the same way God, desiring even more to show to the heirs of the promise the unchangeableness of His purpose, interposed with an oath, in order that by two unchangeable things, in which it is impossible for God to lie, we may have strong encouragement, we who have fled for refuge in laying hold of the hope set before us. This hope we have as an anchor of the soul, a hope both sure and steadfast and one which enters within the veil, where Jesus has entered as a forerunner for us, having become a high priest forever according to the order of Melchizedek (Hebrews 6:13-20).

If you find yourself wearing thin in hope, or starting to wonder if you are going to be able to survive the things life is throwing at you, maybe this booklet will help.

Charles R. Swindoll

Hope

Somewhere along our many miles of Southern California shoreline walked a young, twenty-year-old woman with a terminal disease in her body and a revolver in her hand. She had called me late in the evening and we had talked for a long time. A troubled young woman, her mind was filled with doubts. She had advanced leukemia. The doctors told her she would not live much longer. She checked herself out of a hospital because, as she put it, she "couldn't take another day in that terrible isolation." Her husband had left her; her two-month-old daughter had recently died; her best friend had been killed in an auto accident. Her life was broken. She'd run out of hope. I'll come back to this woman later on.

Doubts often steal into our lives like termites into a house. These termite-like thoughts eat away at our faith. Usually, we can hold up pretty well under this attack. But occasionally, when a strong gale comes along—a sudden, intense blast—we discover we cannot cope. Our house begins to lean. For some people it completely collapses. It is during these stormy times, during the dark days and nights of tragedy and calamity, that we begin to feel the destructive effects of our doubts.

Maximum Pressure Points

For me, there are three times when the intensity of doubt reaches maximum proportions. One such time is when things I believe should never happen, happen.

There are times when my loving, gracious, merciful, kind, good, sovereign God surprises me by saying yes to something I was convinced He would say no to. When bad things happen to good people. When good things happen to bad people. When a lie is passed off as the truth and wins the hearing of the majority.

In his book, *When Bad Things Happen to Good People*, Rabbi Harold Kushner writes:

> There is only one question which really matters: why do bad things happen to good people? All other theological conversation is intellectually diverting. . . . Virtually every meaningful conversation I have ever had with people on the subject of God and religion has either started with this question, or gotten around to it before long. [1]

I once received a letter from a woman who heard over a radio program a talk that I had given entitled, "Riding Out the Storm." Little did she know how meaningful it would be to her, for as she was entering into the truth of that message, she arrived at home only to discover that her young, recently married daughter had been brutally murdered. *Why did God say yes to that?* Why did that bad thing happen to that good person? The effect of such termites within our soul is great. They eat away at us and doubt wins a hearing.

Doubts also increase when things I believe should happen, never happen (the other side of the coin). When I expected God to say yes but He said no. Numerous parents of young men and women have said good-bye and sent their children away to war, convinced that God would bring them home again. But sometimes He says no. How about the family of the policeman who was killed at the onion field outside Bakersfield? Think of their rage as they went the distance to see that the murderers were finally sent to the gas chamber—only to realize the inescapable fact that not only were the killers allowed to live, but one was actually set free.

Joni Eareckson (and a thousand like her) trust confidently for awhile that the paralysis will go away—that God will say, "Yes, I'll get you through this. I'll teach you some deep lessons and then I will use you with full health in days to come as I heal you completely." But God ultimately says no.

Evangelist Leighton Ford and his wife, Jean, members of the Billy Graham Evangelistic Association team, lost their twenty-one-year-old son, Sandy, on November 27, 1981. Four days after the funeral, Ford spoke to the Graham team. His conversation was recorded in part in *Decision* magazine, dated June 1982:

> A week ago yesterday, right before
> Thanksgiving, my stomach was so tied
> up in knots, so anxious that I had to get

out and run. When I stopped, I prayed; I talked with God. I said, "Lord, I know You can heal Sandy through this surgery if You want to. If You don't want to, I can't imagine why You don't." I can't tell you everything I was feeling, but I remember that I finally prayed and said, "God, I just want to say one thing, be good to my boy tomorrow."

I am conscious that almost every one of us has within our hearts—some openly, some secretly—a great gaping, grieving wound that we carry. And in the midst of it we say, "Why? Is God really good?"[2]

That father wanted a yes answer to his prayers. Sandy died. God said no. And he admits:

I would be less than honest if I did not tell you that I wish I could just smile and say, "I'm thankful for this." For there is a part of me inside that says, "It is not right."

. . . I say these things inside myself. They fight. There are hours of great peace and joy, and then there are times when it just closes in, and I say, ". . . Am I doubting God?"[3]

When we expect Him to say yes and He says no, doubts multiply.

There's a third situation where doubts grow. This takes place when things that I believe should happen *now*, happen much, much later. Of all the doubts which "rap and knock and enter in our soul" (Browning), perhaps few are more devastating than those that happen when we are told by God, in effect, "Wait, wait, wait, wait . . . wait . . . wait!" All of us have wrestled greatly with His timing.

These "pressure points" provide a perfect introduction to the verses in Hebrews 6. This is that great chapter that begins with a strong warning, continues with words of affirmation, and closes with words of reassurance and ringing confidence. It addresses the Christian hanging on by his fingernails as he feels himself sliding down the hill. It shouts: "Persevere! Hang tough! Be strong! Don't quit!" Even when God says no and you expected yes. Even when He says yes and you anticipated no. And especially when He says to wait and you expected it now.

A Classic Example: Abraham

. . . when God made the promise to Abraham, since He could swear by no one greater, He swore by Himself, saying, "I will surely bless you, and I will surely multiply you." And thus, having patiently waited, he obtained the promise (vv. 13-15).

What's all that about? Well, maybe we should become acquainted with the warning that comes just before the mention of Abraham. Verse 12 says:

. . . that you may not be sluggish, but imitators of those who through faith and patience inherit the promises.

Imitate those strong-minded men and women in biblical history! They believed God. They said, in effect, "I will stand, no matter what occurs. I will believe God, even though my world crumbles and my house leans. No calamity will make me fall!"

As an illustration of just such an individual, Abraham is mentioned. Now if you don't know your Bible, you can't appreciate the extent to which Abraham and Sarah trusted God. The two of them had been married for years. She was sixty-five; he was seventy-five. And if you can believe this, God had said to the man that in the latter years of his life his wife was going to have a baby. God promised Abraham in no uncertain terms; He swore on the basis of His own integrity that Sarah would have a son. And then, after making that firm promise, God said, "Now you trust Me. You wait."

Abraham waited a year and nothing happened. By then Sarah had turned sixty-six. He waited another ten years and by that time she was seventy-six. Still nothing had happened. *Another* ten years—nothing at all. Then, when Abraham was nearing his one hundredth birthday (which means his wife was about ninety years old), God came back and said, "I'm here again. Guess what? You're still going to have that baby."

If we were to return to the original time when the first dialogue occurred, we would gain a whole new appreciation for God's faithfulness and consistency. It's a wonderful story because it proves how trustworthy God is in the waiting period. Let's pick up the story as God is speaking to His friend, Abraham:

. . . "As for Sarai your wife, you shall not call her name Sarai, but Sarah shall be her name. And I will bless her, and indeed

I will give you a son by her. Then I will
bless her, and she shall be a mother of
nations; kings of peoples shall come from
her. Then Abraham fell on his face and
laughed . . . (Genesis 17:15-17).

Can't you imagine Abraham's response? "Oh,
I cannot believe this. God, here You are talking
about this baby who is going to come into our
home. Oh, God, how can it be? How can it be?" I
love the man's honesty. I wonder if he was smil-
ing, maybe chuckling, when he answered,

. . . "Will a child be born to a man one
hundred years old? And will Sarah, who
is ninety years old, bear a child? . . . Oh
that Ishmael might live before Thee!" (vv.
17-18).

"We have this other young man in our home,
God. Have it happen through him"—that makes
a lot of sense! No, God had not planned that the
arrangement would be through Ishmael. See
verse 19:

. . . "No, but Sarah . . . shall bear you a
son, and you shall call his name
Isaac. . . ."

The name Isaac means *laughter* in Hebrew.
"You laugh at Me; I'll laugh at you. I'll show you
when that boy is born, that I keep My word."

Now you might think Sarah is waiting in the
wings just as confident as she can be that it will
be exactly as it was promised. Better take a close
look at the Genesis account: chapter 18, verse 9.
Three men have come for a visit, bringing the
message from God to underscore what He had
said earlier. Abraham is there; Sarah's listening
through the tent-flap.

. . . "Where is Sarah your wife?" And
he said, "Behold, in the tent." And he said,
"I will surely return to you at this time
next year; and behold, Sarah your wife
shall have a son." And Sarah was listening
at the tent door, which was behind
him. . . . Sarah was past childbearing.
And Sarah laughed to herself . . . (vv. 9-
12).

Ninety years old, why not? There's not much
else to do but laugh at something like that, you
know. After all, "I'm ninety years old and I'm
going to get pregnant? I'm going to bear a son?
You gotta be kidding!"

On our way back to Hebrews 6, let's stop off at
Romans 4. We can't fully appreciate Hebrews or
Genesis without the Romans 4 passage
sandwiched in between. Here's our friend
Abraham who might have laughed on the out-
side, but down deep was obviously confident
God could do it. Romans 4:18:

In hope against hope he believed. . . .

There it is, friends. That's what Hebrews 6 is
talking about. "In hope against hope"—when it
didn't make sense. When the physical body
couldn't pull it off. When it was an impossibility
to man:

. . . in order that he might become a
father of many nations, according to that
which had been spoken, "So shall your
descendants be." And without becoming
weak in faith he contemplated his own
body, now as good as dead since he was
about a hundred years old, and the
deadness of Sarah's womb; yet, with

respect to the promise of God, he did not
waver in unbelief, but grew strong in
faith, giving glory to God, and being fully
assured that what He had promised, He
was able also to perform (Romans 4:18-
21).

That's a clear illustration of faith. That's
believing even when doubts attack. That's being
confident that God knows what He is doing re-
gardless of the waiting period. That's being just
as firm when there's a ten-year period to wait as
when there's only one year ahead. He hoped
against hope:

. . . with respect to the promise of God, he did
not waver in unbelief, but grew strong in faith,
giving glory to God. . . .

That's a very important part of this sentence.
While you wait, you give Him glory. While you
trust Him, you give Him glory. While you accept
the fact that He has you in a holding pattern, you
give Him glory.

. . . Being fully assured that what He
had promised, He was able also to
perform. . . . It was reckoned to him as
righteousness (vv. 21-22).

The man walked patiently through those
years, trusting God.

Trusting . . . in Spite of the Circumstances

Now back to Hebrews 6. This
isn't a lesson on Abraham's life; this is a lesson
for us today. And the lesson has to do with trusting God when things don't work out our way.
This is a lesson on how to deal with doubt. How
to have hope when the answers haven't come.

How to be confident in God when you cannot be confident in your circumstances or your future.

See the transition in verse 16? It all goes back to God's promising on His name that everything would occur just as He promised. Now to bring it into focus, men and women today, the writer adds:

[People today] swear by one greater than themselves, and with them an oath given as confirmation is an end of every dispute (v. 16).

Right hand raised, "Do you swear to tell the truth, the whole truth, and nothing but the truth, so help you God?" You've sworn on One greater than your name, and you are expected in the courtroom to tell the truth. There was none greater, so Almighty God swore on His own name. The writer says in this transitional principle: "Men swear by calling on a name greater than their own name."

In biblical days, before the day of attorneys, title companies, and other modern institutions, people settled their disagreements by coming to a mutual understanding and then confirming it with a promise. Such an oath or promise was final in its authority and settled disputes.

In those days there were many ways to signify that you had negotiated an agreement: You shook hands; or you raised your hand; or you put your thigh next to the thigh of the other person; or you put your hand under the thigh of one who was aged—a number of things were done. But you would swear when you touched the other person that you would do such and such, exactly as you had promised, and it was an oath based on a name greater than your own. Abraham had a promise that was based on God's name; it wouldn't fail. What hope it must have given that old man!

Now, verse 17. Look at how it all ties in:

> In the same way God, desiring even
> more to show to the heirs of the promise
> the unchangeableness of His purpose,
> interposed with an oath. . . .

With God, there is an unchangeable purpose. It is mysterious; it is unfathomable; there is no way, in this point of time, we can unravel all of the reasons behind His purpose. But it *is* unchangeable; it is so firm He has confirmed it by an oath. The passage goes on to say:

> . . . in order that by two unchangeable
> things, in which it is impossible for God
> to lie. . . .

The purpose He has planned for us and the oath He has taken, swearing that that purpose will be unchanged and ultimately right—those two things stand as God's confirmation to His people.

The Need to Think Theologically, Not Logically

I confess to you, at times I doubt God's purpose and promise. I say that to my own embarrassment. When things haven't worked as I thought they would, when I received a no instead of a yes or a yes instead of a no, when I couldn't unravel a situation and fit it with the character of God . . . those have been times when I have said, "I know down inside this isn't right." The writer is coming to us on his knees, saying,

"Please, rather than thinking logically, think *theologically!*" That's awfully good advice.

When the bottom drops out of your life, when hope starts to wear thin, when human logic fails to make much sense, think *theologically!* Go back and read Hebrews 6:17-18. The theological facts are: (1) there is an unchangeable purpose with God; and (2) that purpose is guaranteed with an oath.

It's at this juncture I should add: Don't try to explain it all to someone else. You can't. If you could, you would be God. The only thing you can explain theologically is that it is part of His unchangeable purpose, guaranteed with an oath, neither of which is a lie. That's theological thinking. As Solomon states so well: "[God] has made everything appropriate in its time" (Ecclesiastes 3:11a).

Let me give you a syllogism—a theological syllogism:

God is in control of the times and
seasons.
Some times are hard and some seasons
are dry.

So the conclusion is:

God is in control of hard times and dry
seasons.

We are quick to give God praise when the blessings flow—when the checking account is full and running over; when the job is secure, and a promotion is on the horizon; when the salary is good; when our health is fine. But we have a tough time believing when those things aren't true.

Three Benefits of Thinking Theologically

There are benefits that come from thinking theologically; you'll see three of them right here in these two verses in Hebrews 6. Look at verse 18:

> . . . by two unchangeable things, in which it is impossible for God to lie, we may have strong encouragement. . . .

Logical thinking will discourage you; theological thinking will encourage you. That's the first benefit . . . *personal encouragement.* Believe it. You will have "strong encouragement."

Read on:

> . . . we who have fled for refuge in laying hold of the hope. . . .

That's the second benefit . . . *a refuge of hope.* Encouragement is the opposite of discouragement. Hope is the opposite of despair. When you accept the fact that sometimes seasons are dry and times are hard and that God is in control of both, you will discover a sense of divine refuge, because the hope then is in God and not in yourself. That explains why Abraham gave glory to God during the waiting period. "I can't figure it out, I cannot explain it, but Lord, You promised me . . . and I give You glory for the period of waiting, even though I'm getting up in years."

A strong encouragement, a refuge of hope, and for the ultimate benefit, read on:

> This hope we have as an anchor of the soul. . . .

That's the third benefit . . . *an anchor for the soul.* The word "anchor" is used often in ancient literature, but it is only used once in the New

Testament, right here in Hebrews 6. There are lots of hymns and gospel songs that make use of the anchor metaphor. Every one of them comes back to this verse that refers to the "anchor of the soul."

There's something beautiful in this word picture that I would have missed without the advice of one very capable scholar:

> The picture is that of an ancient sailing vessel finding its way through the narrow entrance to a harbor. This was one of the trickiest maneuvers the captain of a ship had to make. As his ship moved through the opening, he had to guard against a gust of wind running it onto a reef or a sandbar. The skeleton of many a ship could be seen on the rocks, giving testimony to the fact that its captain had failed his navigation test.
>
> To minimize the risk, the olden-day skipper would lower the ship's anchor into a smaller boat, which would then be rowed through the narrow entrance of the harbor. The anchor would then be dropped and this ship, with sails down, would be pulled past the obstacles, through the narrow opening, and into the safety of the harbor.[4]

I distinctly remember when our troop ship arrived (after seventeen days at sea!) at the harbor city of Yokohama, Japan. As we approached the harbor, the skipper stopped our ship and it sat silent in the deep sea, like an enormous, bloated whale. We marines waited on the deck in the hot sunshine as a tiny tugboat left the harbor and came out toward our huge vessel. Soon, a small Japanese gentleman came up the side of our ship and ultimately took the controls of our ship as he personally guided it until we were safely docked in the harbor. Someone later explained the reason to me: There were still mines in the Japanese harbor. That's a fun thought after seventeen days at sea: "Welcome to Japan; the mines are ready for you!" He guided us through the treacherous waters of the harbor and right up to the pier.

The Spiritual Analogy

The point of all of this, of course, is not anchors and skippers, ships and harbors. The point is this: That is *exactly* what Jesus Christ does when the bottom of life drops out. Look closely at the verse:

> . . . We have as an anchor of the soul, a
> hope both sure and steadfast and one
> which enters within the veil. . . .

The imagery of that verse may not be clear at first glance. Let me put it in today's terms. In the days of the Tabernacle, the Jews gathered around it and within it as a place of worship. Within the Tabernacle were veils; within the innermost veil was the holiest place on earth . . . the place we might call the "God-room." In this God-room the light (or, as it was called, the *shekinah*) of God resided. It's my understanding that the light of God was a brilliant, blazing light that shone down into the God-room. Within that room was an ark, or a small chest, much lower and smaller than most pulpits. On top of that chest was a grail, with golden cherubim on either end (angel-like creatures with their wings folded in front of them). That entire piece of unique furniture was too holy for words.

Once a year the high priest of the Jews would enter that God-room with a small pan of blood which, precisely as God required it in the Law, he poured out on the grail (which was called the "mercy seat") there between the golden cherubim. God, witnessing the spilling of the blood and pleased with the sacrifice that had been made correctly by the priest, graciously forgave the Jewish people. It was an annual event; it was the most sacred of all events. The Hebrews must have held their breath as the high priest went in with the pan, poured the blood, and came out of this room where God dwelled. The first-century Jews who read this word "veil" in Hebrews 6 understood all that. Look closely:

This hope we have as an anchor . . . a hope both sure and steadfast . . . one which enters within the veil, where Jesus has entered as a forerunner for us, having become a high priest forever according to the order of Melchizedek (vv. 19-20).

In other words, our Savior has gone through life, has taken all of life's beatings and buffetings, and He has gone before us. And now? Now He pulls us toward Himself! He invites His followers within the veil. He says, "Come in. Find here the rest that you need, the relief from the burdens and buffetings of doubt."

Doubt, you see, will always try to convince you, "You are all alone. No one else knows. Or cares. No one else really can enter in and help you with this." In Hebrews, however, the writer says that Christ is our constant priest—not once a year, but forever. He lives in the God-room. He is there, sitting alongside the Father, representing your needs to Him. And, child of God, there is nothing so great for you to endure that He does not feel touched by it and stay by you through it.

Some Pertinent and Practical Reminders

Now I want to say very practically, when you minister to people who have come to the end of their trail of despair, *logic won't cut it.* Logical thinking will not help you, nor will it help them. Sometimes, quite honestly, it will backfire. I'll give you an illustration:

Writer Harriet Sarnoff Schiff has distilled her pain and tragedy in a book called *The Bereaved Parent.* She remembers that when her young son died during an operation to correct a congenital heart malfunction, her clergyman took her aside and said, "I know that this is a painful time for you. But I know that you will get through it all right, because God never sends us more of a burden than we can bear. God only let this happen to you because He knows that you are strong enough to handle it." Harriet Schiff remembers her reaction to those words: "If only I was a weaker person, Robbie would still be alive."[5]

Human logic, you see, breaks down. The mystery is enormous. And it is the enormity of it all that calls for faith. I'm sorry if that sounds like an overused bromide. But if we could unravel it, why would we need faith? If that were true, all we'd really need is the answer in the back of the book and someone to point it out to us; we'd read it and that's all there would be to it. But God's plan is that we walk by faith, *not* by sight. It is faith and patience that stretch us to the breaking point. Such things send doubt running.

When you find yourself dealing with doubt, let me give you three things to remember. First, *God cannot lie.* He can test, and He will. He can say no, and He sometimes will; He can say yes, and He will; He can say "wait," and occasionally He will—but God cannot lie. He must keep His word. Doubt says, "You fool, you're stupid to believe in a God who puts you through this." By faith, keep remembering that God cannot lie.

I appreciate very much the words of one survivor of Auschwitz:

It never occurred to me to question God's doings or lack of doings while I was an inmate of Auschwitz. Although, of course, I understand others did. I was no less or no more religious because of what the Nazis did to us, and I believe my faith in God was not undermined in the least. It never occurred to me to associate the calamity we were experiencing with God, to blame Him, or to believe in Him less, or cease believing in Him at all because He didn't come to our aid. God doesn't owe us that, or anything. We owe our lives to Him. If someone believes God is responsible for the death of six million because He didn't somehow do something to save them, he's got his thinking reversed. We owe God our lives for the few or many years we live. And we have the duty to worship Him and do as He commands. That's what we're here on earth for; to be in God's service and to do God's bidding.[6]

God cannot lie.

Here's the second piece of advice that helps me: *We will not lose.* Doubt says, "You lose if you trust God through this. You lose." If I read anything in this whole section of Hebrews 6, I read that in the mysterious manner of God's own timing, for some unexplainable and yet unchangeable purpose, those of us who trust Him ultimately win—because God ultimately wins.

There's a little chorus that Christians love to sing. It is quiet and tender, yet tough and true:

In His time, in His time,
He makes all things beautiful
In His time.

Lord, please show me every day,
As You're teaching me Your way,
That You do just what You say,
In Your time.[7]

God cannot lie. We will not lose. Your mate has walked away from you, an unfair departure—you will not lose, child of God. Your baby has been born and for some reason it has been chosen to be one of those special persons on this earth. You will not lose. You've waited and waited, and you were convinced that things would improve, yet things have only gotten worse—keep remembering, you will not lose. God swears on it with an oath that cannot change. You will not lose.

Third—and I guess it's the best of all—is that *our Lord Jesus does not leave.* To quote a verse from Scripture, He "sticks closer than a brother" (Proverbs 18:24).

. . . Jesus has entered as a forerunner for us, having become a high priest forever . . . (Hebrews 6:20).

That means He is there at any time . . . and always.

Remember the young woman I mentioned earlier? Remember her difficult circumstances? Advanced leukemia, daughter dead, husband gone, greater debt than she could even add up. She had checked herself out of a hospital, deciding that anything would be better than the isolation she was in as she endured that advanced stage of leukemia.

She and I spoke calmly and quietly about what was happening. I did a lot of listening. There were periods when there was silence on the phone for thirty to forty-five seconds. I didn't know where she was. I still don't know her full name. She spoke of taking her husband's revolver and going out on the beach to finish it all, and she asked me a lot of questions about suicide.

In what seemed an inappropriate moment . . . I felt peace, a total absence of panic. I had no fear that she would hang up and take her life. I simply spoke very, very quietly about her future. I made no special promise that she would immediately be healed. I knew that she might not live much longer, as her doctors were talking to her in terms of a very few weeks—perhaps days. I spoke to her about Christ and the hope He could provide. After a sigh and with an ache that was obvious, she hung up.

It was about thirty minutes later that the phone rang again. It was the same young woman. She had a friend who was a nurse, who used to come to our church in Fullerton, California. The nurse had given her a New Testament in which she had written my name and phone number and had said, "If you really are in deep need, I think he will understand." By the way, the nurse—her closest friend—was the one who had been killed in the auto accident. She had nothing to cling to from that friendship but memories and this Testament. She read from it. I said, "What does it say to you?" She said, "Well, I think the first part of it is biography and the last part is a group of letters that explain how to do what's in that biography." (That's a good analysis of the New Testament.) I said, "Have you done that?" And she had called back to say, "Yes, I've done that. I decided, Chuck, that I would, without reservation, give myself to Jesus Christ. I'm still afraid; I still have doubts. I still don't know what tomorrow's going to bring, but I want you to know that I have turned my life over to Jesus and I'm trusting Him through this. He has given me new hope . . . the one thing I really needed."

It's very possible that someone reading these words right now feels the very same way. You're thinking thoughts that you have never entertained before, and you're thinking them more often and more seriously. Without trying to use any of the clichés on you, I would say that this hope Christ can bring, this "anchor of the soul," is the only way through. I have no answer other than Jesus Christ. I can't promise you healing, nor can I predict that your world will come back right side up. But I *can* promise you that He will receive you as you come in faith to Him. And He will bring back the hope you need so desperately. The good news is this: That hope will not only get you through this particular trial, it will ultimately take you "within the veil" when you die.

Father, it is my desire to give You praise even when bad things happen to good people. Even when the end seems terribly premature. And when I hear a no though I expected a yes . . . or a yes when I was so sure of a no . . . or "wait" when I was confident of "now." When the doubts storm in to blight my faith and tempt me to question Your integrity, help me, Father! Only You can do that, like You did for Abraham and Sarah, who waited twenty-five long years for the fulfillment of a single promise. Help us not to stagger in unbelief but, like Abraham, to trust You through times of doubt.

In the name of Christ, the Giver of hope, the permanent Priest, I pray. Amen.

---

[1]Harold S. Kushner, *When Bad Things Happen to Good People* (New York: Schocken Books, 1981), p. 6.

[2]Leighton Ford, "Yes, God Is Good," *Decision*, June 1982, p. 5.

[3]Ibid.

[4]Walter A. Henrichsen, *After the Sacrifice* (Grand Rapids: Zondervan Publishing House, 1979), p. 83.

[5]Kushner, *When Bad Things Happen to Good People*, p. 26.

[6]Source unknown.

[7]From the song "In His Time" by Diane Ball, © 1978 by Maranatha Music. All rights reserved. International copyright secured. Used by permission.